This book may be returned to any Wiltshire
library. To renew this book phone your library
or visit the website: www.wiltshire.gov.uk

M
Macmillan Education
London and Basingstoke

First published 1976

Reprinted 1977 (twice), 1978, 1979, 1981, 1982 (twice)

Published by
MACMILLAN EDUCATION LIMITED
Houndmills, Basingstoke, Hampshire RG21 2XS
and London

Associated companies in Delhi Dublin
Hong Kong   Johannesburg   Lagos   Melbourne
New York   Singapore   and   Tokyo

Printed in Hong Kong

FOREWORD

DRAMASCRIPTS are intended for use in secondary schools, amateur
theatrical groups and youth clubs, and some will be enjoyed by young
people who are still at primary school. They may be used in a variety of
ways: read privately for pleasure or aloud in groups; acted in the classroom,
church hall or youth club, or in public performances.

The adventures of TOM SAWYER and his friends have fascinated
young people—and millions of adults—ever since Mark Twain created his
immortal classic in 1875. Tom's brushes with his strict but human Aunt
Polly, his escapades with Huckleberry Finn in the graveyard at midnight,
his pirating capers with Huck and Joe, and the boys' sudden reappearance,
alive, at their own funeral service—all these exciting and sometimes
hilariously funny episodes are neatly reconstructed here in a form in which
they will be readily appreciated.

GUY WILLIAMS
Advisory Editor

THE CHARACTERS

AUNT POLLY, Tom's guardian
TOM SAWYER
SID SAWYER, Tom's brother
BEN ROGERS, friend of Tom Sawyer
HUCK FINN, orphan friend of Tom Sawyer
JOE HARPER, friend of Tom Sawyer
BECKY THATCHER, Tom's current girlfriend and daughter of Judge
    Thatcher
MUFF POTTER, 'an old reprobate' and friend of Tom Sawyer
MINISTER, The Reverend Peterson
INJUN JOE, a cunning Indian
DR ROBINSON
SHERIFF
PEOPLE IN THE CROWD: FIVE MEN
                     TWO WOMEN
JUDGE THATCHER
SCHOOLMASTER, Mr Snodgrass, a sombre man
AMY LAWRENCE ⎱
JOSIE PRESTON ⎰ classmates of Tom Sawyer
MRS HARPER, Joe Harper's mother
BILL THOMSON, Injun Joe's partner in crime
MINISTER'S WIFE
WIDOW DOUGLAS, Huck Finn's sometime patron
MRS THATCHER, the Judge's wife
MR HARPER, Joe Harper's father
THREE MEN, friends of Injun Joe
Girls, boys, women and men for crowd scenes

The action of this play takes place in and around the little town of
St Petersburg on the Mississippi river.

ACT ONE

Scene 1

(A back street running between **Aunt Polly's** *house and the* **Thatchers'** *house. The fence of* **Aunt Polly's** *house runs about half the width of the stage.*

The stage is empty. There is a shout of 'Tom Sawyer!' **Tom** *leaps over the fence and hides behind a barrel.* **Aunt Polly** *appears on the porch and looks around for him.)*

Aunt Polly. Tom! Tom Sawyer! Where's that boy gone I wonder? I do declare. . . . *(She waves her switch)* If I lay hold of him I'll flay his hide!

*(***Tom** *begins to creep away on hands and knees, when* **Sid** *peers over the fence and sees him)*

Sid. Here he is, Aunt Polly. Here he is.

Aunt Polly *(Rushing out of the garden gate and seizing him by his trousers).* Ah, got you, sir! The door of the jam closet is open. Do you know that?

Tom. No, Aunt Polly.

Aunt Polly. What you been up to in there?

Tom. Why, nothin'.

Aunt Polly. Nothin'? Look at your lips. Look at your fingers. What is that if it ain't jam? Don't answer me one word! Just you take off your jacket. If I've warned you once about that jam I've warned you forty times.

Tom. Honest, Aunt Polly.

Aunt Polly. Off with it, I said!

1

(Aunt Polly raises her stick and pushes Tom's head down)

Tom. Look behind you!

(Aunt Polly jumps round and lifts up her skirts. Tom disappears behind the Thatchers' fence.)

Aunt Polly. Hang the boy! Can't I ever learn anythin'—ain't he played me enough tricks fer me to be lookin' out fer him? Ah, well, they say old fools is the biggest fools there is, and he never plays the same trick twice!

(Aunt Polly goes into the garden, shaking her head. As she turns for a last look around she sees Tom sneaking off. She marches back through the garden gate and grabs him.)

Tom, Tom! You seem to try an' break my old heart just every way you can. I ought to switch you good fer stealin' jam, but you're my own sister's child and I ain't the heart to lash you.

Tom. I won't take any more of that jam, Aunt.

Aunt Polly. You mean that, Tom?

Tom. Sure, Aunt. There ain't any more. I've et it!

Aunt Polly. Oh, I'm neglectin' my duty not to switch you good. It's no use. I'll be obleeged to set you to work to punish you. YOU'll whitewash this fence before you take one step to play!

Tom. Aunt Polly! It's Saturday.

Aunt Polly. I promised your poor mother I'd do my duty to you, and so I will.

Tom. I'd rather be licked. I'd rather take a thousand lickin's. *(He bends over)* Here, Aunt Polly. Hit me. I won't run away. There ain't anyone behind you this time.

Aunt Polly. No! I ain't goin' to back down. It's hard to make you work on a holiday, but maybe it'll do you more good than a lickin'!

Tom. Not now, Aunt. Anytime but now!

Sid *(Over the garden fence).* I know what's eatin' him, Aunt Polly. He's waitin' for Becky Thatcher to finish her music lesson. I heard 'em talkin' while I was weedin' the garden.

Tom. I'll lick yer for that, Sid!

2

Aunt Polly. Shame, Tom. Speakin' to your own brother like that!

Tom. I promised Becky, Aunt. I can't break my word, can I?

Sid. You ought to have heard him puttin' on airs when she said she had a music lesson on a Saturday! 'I'd like to see anyone make me work on a holiday.' That's how he went on, Aunt.

Aunt Polly. Oh, he said that, did he? We'll see about that! Sid, you just fetch me the whitewash pail and brushes.

Sid. Sure, Aunt Polly!

(Sid goes into the house)

Tom. It's goin' to take all afternoon. I've promised to meet Joe an' Huck at four sharp.

Aunt Polly. I've told you before you're to have no truck with that Huck Finn! It ain't respectable the way he sleeps out at night and scavenges for food like an alley cat. He ain't no example fer a respectable boy to follow.

Tom. It isn't Huck's fault, Aunt Polly. You know that. He ain't got a father or a mother nor any kin . . . . An', besides, Muff Potter's promised to show us a new fishin' hole.

Aunt Polly. That settles it, Tom Sawyer! I won't have you associatin' with that old reprobate. He's a drunkard and a gambler and . . . and a general no good layabout. He ain't fit fer boys to be runnin' after.

Tom. He's waitin' fer me!

Aunt Polly. You're not goin' to stir from this yard 'til you get through whitewashin' that fence.

Tom. If I'm not there on time they'll go without me. Then they'll laugh at me an' crow over me!

Sid *(Entering with pail and brushes).* Here's the pail, Aunt Polly.

Aunt Polly. Thankee, Sidney. Pick up the brush, Tom, and get started.

Tom *(Holding up the brush).* This brush won't work, Aunt Polly. See! It's all stiff. I guess I can't whitewash after all.

Aunt Polly *(Examining the brush).* I guess you're right, Tom. . . .

Sid *(Producing a brush from behind his back).* I brought this one for

3

you, Tom. It's new.

Aunt Polly. Good boy, Sidney. Run along and play.

*(*Sid *goes off, grinning at* Tom*)*

Tom *(Calling after* Sid*).* I'll lick yer for that, little mister smartypants! See if I don't!

Aunt Polly. Shame on you, Tom Sawyer! Suppose Becky heard you?

Tom. Shucks! Who cares what girls think? Thin-skinned and chicken-hearted.

Aunt Polly. Get to work now. See if you can't be a good boy for once.

(**Aunt Polly** *goes out)*

Tom *(Sitting on the barrel).* Blame it! That's torn everythin'!

Ben *(Off-stage).* Tom! Tom Sawyer! Where are you?

Tom *(Thinking desperately).* By jingo! . . . No . . . . It might work at that!

(**Tom** *seizes the brush and begins to whitewash vigorously)*

Ben *(Comes in eating a large, red apple).* Hi Tom!

(There is no reply)

I said 'Hi, Tom'.

Tom. Oh . . . hello, Ben!

(**Tom** *carries on whitewashing)*

Ben. What you doin'?

Tom. Whitewashin'.

Ben. Too bad. On a holiday, too. Me an' the boys are goin' fishin' with Muff Potter. Don't you wish you could come?

Tom. I kin fish any old day of the week.

Ben. Course, you'd rather work.

Tom. What d'you call work?

Ben. Ain't that work?

Tom. Mebbe it is . . . and, again, mebbe it ain't.

Ben. You ain't tryin' to let on you *likes* it?

Tom. I don't see why I oughtn't to like it. A fellow doesn't get the chance to whitewash a fence every day.

(**Tom** *carries on whitewashing*)

Ben *(After a moment).* Say, lemme whitewash awhile, Tom.

Tom. No, Ben.

Ben. Why not?

Tom. I'm sorry, Ben, but it wouldn't do.

Ben. Why wouldn't it?

Tom. Aunt Polly's awful particular about this here fence. If it were only the back fence ... well, I might let you have a go. But it's the front fence, and bang opposite Judge Thatcher's, an' it's got to be done just so.

Ben. I'll be careful, Tom.

Tom. I reckon there ain't one boy in a thousand can do this fence as it ought to be done. Sid wanted to do it, but Aunt Polly said 'no'. She said, 'Tom's the only one I can trust.'

Ben. That so? Well, lemme try. Just a little. If you was me I'd let you, Tom.

Tom. I can't, Ben. If I was to let you tackle this fence an' anythin' went wrong, I don't know what she'd do to me. She's an awful hard woman when she's angered, Ben.

Ben. I'll give you the core of my apple.

Tom. No, Ben. I'm afeerd.

Ben. I'll give you all of it. Look, it ain't more'n half chewed!

Tom *(Handing him the brush).* Well, try Ben. I'll keep an eye on it . . . and mind those drips.

(**Ben** *begins to whitewash while* **Tom** *sits on the barrel and begins to eat the apple. A whistle is heard off-stage.* **Tom** *grabs the other brush and begins to instruct* **Ben***)*

Slap it on free, Ben. Like this. Then finish up nice an' careful . . . so.

5

(Huck and Joe enter. Huck is swinging a dead cat by the tail. They watch with growing envy.)

Joe. Hi, Tom!

Tom. Hello, Joe.

Huck. Hi, Tom!

Tom. Hi, Huck.

Joe. What you two doin'? I thought we were goin' with Muff Potter to that new fishin' place?

Tom *(Ignoring them).* It's not bad, Ben. Not bad at all.

Ben. Mine's as smooth as yours!

Tom. Not quite, Ben, not quite, but I reckon it'll pass. I don't reckon Aunt Polly'll notice anythin' amiss.

Joe. Lemme take a whack at it!

Huck. No, lemme!

Joe. I'll give you this piece of blue glass to look through.

Huck. An' I'll give you a marble an' two fish hooks an' a key!

(Huck lays them on the barrel)

Tom. What does it unlock?

Huck. Nothin'! But it's a *genwine* key.

Tom. I don't know, Huck . . . .

Joe. I'll go get my kite from off Muff Potter. He's down at the town pump. Then will you give me a try at the fence?

Tom. Depends on the kite. I might.

(Joe goes out)

Huck. Well, Tom, is it a deal?

Tom. I don't know, Huckleberry. Say, what's that you got?

Huck. This? Dead cat.

Tom. Say, he's a beauty. Where'd you get him?

Huck. Bought him off'n a boy. I gave a hoop, an' a licris stick, an' a

6

sheep's bladder I hooked from the slaughter house. This is a pretty expensive cat.

Tom *(Prodding it).* He's stiff as a board.

Huck. So'd you be if you'd bin dead three days.

Tom. What is dead cats good fer, Huck?

Huck. Cure warts.

Tom. How'd they do that, Huck?

Huck. I thought most everyone knew! You take your cat an' hit out fer the graveyard, an' look about fer a grave where someone wicked's bin buried that very day. When it's midnight a devil'll come . . . maybe more'n one . . . only you can't hear or see 'em, you can only hear somethin' like the wind moanin'! Then—on the stroke of midnight when they're takin' him away—you heave the cat after them an' say . . . 'Devil follow body, cat follow devil, warts follow cat.' Then you light off home an' don't tell anyone, 'cause if you do the charm's busted. That ought to fetch any wart.

Tom. When you goin' to try the cat, Huck?

Huck. They buried old Hoss Williams today. They say he was real wicked. I reckon the devil'll be after him tonight.

Tom. Lemme go with you, Huck?

Huck. Lemme whitewash?

Tom. It's a deal!

Joe *(Dashing in with the kite).* Here's the kite! Now kin I have a brush?

Tom *(Inspecting the kite).* Yes, Joe, I reckin this is worth a while if you're careful. *(He gives* Huck *and* Joe *a brush)* Now, git goin'! Try to keep in time. One, two . . . one, two. Good, wide strokes. That's better.

Huck. This is a whack!

Joe. It's gay!

Ben. I sure like this.

Tom *(Who has been lolling on the barrel suddenly sees something off-stage).* You men start on the other side now. I'll stay an' watch this side dries right.

Huck. We ain't done yet.

Joe. I'd rather stay over here.

Tom. Whose fence is this, anyway? Don't you want to whitewash anymore?

Joe. We'll do the other side if you say so. Come on Huck, Ben.

Tom. Don't fergit the pail!

(Ben, Huck and Joe all go round the other side of the fence. After a moment Becky appears through her garden. She sees Tom, who seems to be busy whittling a piece of wood.)

Becky. That's pretty.

Tom. Why, Becky! I didn't hear you come out.

Becky. I've brought the pencil and paper.

Tom. Good. *(He brings the barrel forward)* This'll do as a table.

Becky. Couldn't we go on our porch? It's cooler there.

Tom. I told a few of the boys to whitewash Aunt Polly's fence, so I have to keep an eye on 'em. Just wait 'til I see how they're doin' will you? *(He leans over the fence)* That's not too bad, Joe. You too, Huck. Take care down at the bottom there, Ben. We don't want whitewash spillin' over the flowers. Aunt Polly's awful proud of her petunias.

Huck. We're takin' good care, Tom.

Tom *(Strolling back to* **Becky***).* I guess they're doin' all right. What you writin'? *(She gives him a piece of paper)* 'Thomas Sawyer'. That's the name Aunt Polly gives me when she licks me. When I'm good I'm Tom. You kin call me Tom, Becky.

Becky. Now show me how to draw a house.

Tom *(Guiding her hand over the paper).* Say, Becky . . . .

Becky. What?

Tom. Were you ever engaged?

Becky. What's that?

Tom. Why, you just get engaged.

Becky. I don't think so.

Tom. Well, would you like to?

Becky. I don't know. I reckon so. What's it like?

Tom. It ain't *like* anythin'! You just tell a boy you'll be engaged to him. And goin' home and comin' to school I'll walk along with you, and maybe even carry your satchel.

Becky. Is that all?

Tom. And at parties, you choose me an' I'll choose you, because that's the way you do when you're engaged.

Becky. It sounds nice. I never heard of it before.

Tom. Will you, Becky?

Becky. I don't know.

Tom. Yes, you do. Tell me.

Becky. Not now. Tomorrow.

Tom. Oh, no! Now. Please, Becky!

*(***Becky*** gets up and runs to the garden gate)*

Becky. 'Byem' bye, Tom.

Tom. Becky! Maybe at four o'clock?

*(***Joe*** looks over the fence)*

Joe. We're through in here. Come an' look.

Ben. It's bully!

Huck. You come an' see.

Tom. How about that corner, Joe?

Joe. Oh, we did that long ago. Ain't that right, Huck?

Huck. Sure thing, Joe!

Tom. Just you carry on fer a minute and then I'll come and see.

Joe. Sure, Tom.

(Their heads disappear and they continue working)

*(***Becky*** bends to pick a flower from her garden. She throws it over*

9

the fence to **Tom** *and then disappears indoors.* **Tom** *picks it up, and is fixing it in his button hole when* **Muff Potter** *appears. He approaches* **Tom** *from behind and places a hand on his shoulder.)*

Muff. I thought we was goin' fishin', young feller!

(At the sound of his voice **Huck,** **Joe** *and* **Ben** *pop their heads up over the fence)*

What are ye all up to now?

Joe. We're givin' Tom a hand whitewashin', Muff.

Huck. We kin go now, though. It's done.

(They troop out to the front of the fence)

Muff. Let's git started then.

Tom. I can't start 'til four, Muff.

Muff. That's 'til late. Why, we wouldn't git back 'til supper. Then what would your aunt say? She'd lick yer!

Tom. Aunt Polly never licks no one!

Muff. An' she'd heap coals o' fire on my head fer keepin' you out late! I don't intend to cross your aunt, Tom. I've had the sharp end of her tongue afore now. I reckon we'd better call if off 'til another day.

Joe. Aw! Now Muff . . . .

Muff. I told you I'd have to make an early start. I've certain plans laid for tonight, and I've got to get ready fer 'em.

Huck. What you plannin', Muff?

Ben. Is it more important than us?

Muff. You'll keep. It won't. It's a man's work an' it's got to be done tonight. Well, boys, I'll be seein' yer.

*(***Muff*** goes out)*

Huck. There goes our fishin'.

Tom. It's almost four o'clock, anyway.

Aunt Polly *(From indoors).* No, you can't have another doughnut, Sidney. You've et four already, and I do declare if you eat one more you'll be sick!

10

Tom. You boys better scat. If Aunt Polly knew you'd messed with this 'ere fence she wouldn't like it.

*(*Huck, Ben *and* Joe *disappear.* Aunt Polly *comes through the garden, followed by* Sid.*)*

Aunt Polly. Thomas Sawyer! What are you sittin' idle for when there's work to be done? I was aimin' to give you the rest of these dough-nuts, but you don't git a bite 'til you finish your job!

Tom. It's all finished, Aunt Polly.

Aunt Polly. Now don't you lie to me, Thomas Sawyer! I know . . . . *(She catches sight of the fence)* Well, I never! There's no gettin' around it. You kin work when you've a mind to.

(The Minister *passes by, and stops to admire the fence)*

Minister. Good afternoon, Miss Sawyer.

Aunt Polly. Good afternoon, Reverend!

Minister. My, it's a long time since I saw a fence with such a fine fresh coat of whitewash!

Aunt Polly. It's my Tom's handiwork.

Minister. And on a Saturday, too! Where are all your little playmates?

Tom. They went fishin'.

Minister. And you chose to stay at home and complete this noble task for the love of work well done! Such an example of devotion to duty is an example to us all. Such industry in a lad of your years cheers my heart. Let me shake your hand my boy.

*(*Tom *transfers the whitewash brush to his left hand, and shakes hands with the* Minister. *In doing so he leaves a smear of whitewash on his gloves. The* Minister *withdraws his hand hastily.)*

Good afternoon, ma'am.

(He raises his hat and departs)

Aunt Polly. Here, Tom, have a doughnut. Take two—and don't let me catch you tryin' to hook any more.

*(*Aunt Polly *puts the bowl down and turns to examine the fence)*

Tom. Thanks, Aunt Polly.

(Tom takes a doughnut. **Sid** *makes a grab for the bowl, but knocks it over.* **Tom** *catches him a blow on the ear and* **Sid** *makes off. As* **Tom** *bends to pick up the doughnuts* **Aunt Polly** *turns and, thinking he is stealing them, clouts him on the side of the head.)*

What you hittin' me for? It was Sid knocked 'em over.

Aunt Polly. Well, I reckon if you didn't deserve it this time you soon will.

*(***Aunt Polly*** *takes up the bowl and makes her way into the house.* **Tom** *rubs his ear. He sits on the barrel and pulls a glass doorknob from his pocket, and squints at his reflection in it.* **Becky** *comes out of her garden gate.)*

Becky. What you got there, Tom?

Tom. Hello, Becky. D'you like it?

Becky. Sure I do. What is it?

Tom. Why, it's a glass doorknob. Solid crystal. Look, you kin see a live rainbow in it.

*(***Becky*** *looks into the doorknob)*

Becky. Why, so you can! It's the prettiest thing I ever did see.

Tom. Would you like it?

Becky. You mean . . . . you'd give it me, Tom?

Tom. Sure I will, Becky. If you say you'll be engaged to me.

Becky. Then I'll be engaged, Tom.

Tom. Take it. *(He gives it to her)* Here, have a doughnut, too.

Becky. Thanks. I just love doughnuts.

Tom. Tomorrow I'll hook plenty more when Aunt Polly isn't lookin'; an' after school I'll meet you an' we kin sit in the swings and eat 'em!

Becky. Oh, that sounds nice!

Tom. It's gay! Why, I remember when me an' Amy Lawrence was engaged we . . . .

Becky. Amy Lawrence!

*(***Becky*** *turns away sobbing)*

12

Tom. I don't like her any more.

Becky. Yes, you do! You know you do!

Tom. I don't! Honest I don't, Becky.

Becky. Take your old doorknob. I don't want it.

(Becky thrusts it back into his hand)

Tom. It's the nicest thing I got, Becky. I wouldn't give it to any other girl but you.

Becky. You can keep it, Thomas Sawyer—and your doughnut. I never want to speak to you again.

(Becky flounces off)

Tom. Becky! Come back! Aw, what's the use? She'll be sorry some day. They'll all be sorry when it's too late.

(Tom slumps on the barrel. Huck and Joe come in.)

Joe. Hi, Tom!

Tom. Hi, Joe. Hi, Huck.

Huck. What's the matter, Tom? You ain't ill, are you?

Tom. When I'm gone, don't you forgit me, will you? I'm goin' away.

Joe. Why, Tom?

Tom. Everyone's agin me. Aunt Polly belted me 'cause she thought I stole a doughnut, an' it was Sid took it. Nobody loves me.

Joe. Same here, Tom. I just went in an' my mother laid into me with a broom fer drinkin' cream I don't rightly know nothin' about. Didn't give me a chance to explain.

Tom. I try to do right like the Minister's allus tellin' us, but they won't let me. Right, I'll go. When they find out I've gone, an' they've driven me to it, perhaps they'll be sorry.

Joe. Same with me, Tom. My parents don't 'preciate me. I'll come with you.

Tom. What about you, Huck? You goin' to run away too?

Huck. I ain't got no parents or r'latives to run away from, Tom. Still, I reckon I'll come along.

13

Tom. That's bully!

Huck. Where are we goin'?

(They think for a moment)

Tom. I know. I'm goin' to be a pirate.

Huck. What do pirates do?

Tom. Geewhillikins, Huck, did you never have no education?

Huck. No. Lestways, the widder Douglas tried to edicate me, but it didn't work out. She made me sleep in a bed an' wear shoes an' took away my baccy an' pipe. Why, she even tried to make me wash every day . . . an' twice on Sundays. I reckoned it weren't healthy so I lit out an' left.

Tom. Anyway, pirates sail the seven seas an' take ships an' burn 'em, an' have heaps of treasure an' bury it on their island.

Huck. Sounds just fine!

Tom. Hand me that cat, Huck. *(He places it on the barrel)* Put your hand on mine, Joe. You too, Huck. Now . . . 'We swear to stand by each other, an' never separate from each other "til death".' That's the oath. All pirates have 'em.

Joe. That's bully, Tom.

Tom. We got to have a countersign.

Joe. I know—blood!

All. BLOOD!!

Huck. Then we got to have an island.

Tom. Jackson's Island'll do fine. It's right handy.

Huck. It's no size for a pirate island. Anyway, it's only three miles up river.

Joe. Two.

Tom. Well, we can make out it's three, can't we? We've got to start small.

Huck. Say! I know where there's an old raft nobody owns. We could most likely repair it in under a day.

Tom. Could we do it by midnight?

14

Huck. What about the graveyard?

Tom. Shucks, I clean forgot about that. Tell you what. We'll all go to the graveyard tonight . . . .

Joe. Not me!

Tom. Why not?

Joe. 'Cause I'm skeered, that's why.

Tom. If you don't want to help us look fer treasure to take to our island, you don't have to. You'll look mighty small when Huck an' me are swaggerin' about with . . . with diamond rings as big as your eye on our fingers.

Joe. Where you aimin' to look fer this . . . buried treasure?

Tom. You kin look in haunted houses, sometimes, or sometimes on islands, but mostly under the end of a dead limb tree where the shadow falls at midnight.

Huck. Why, Tom, there's a dead limb tree plumb outside the gate of the cemetry.

Tom. Come on, Huck. No time to waste. Perhaps we'll find a brass pot full of diamonds, or a rotten chest just burstin' with silver dollars.

Huck. I'm with you, Tom.

Joe. I'm not strikin' up an acquaintance with no old devils in that graveyard. No, sir! But I'll come after midnight an' help you dig.

Tom. I reckon we might need you to carry the treasure.

Joe. I'll see what I kin hook in the way of food from home, then we kin have a feed after we're through diggin'.

Tom. Ain't it a good idea?

Huck. It's bully!

Joe. It's the best!

Huck. What names shall we have? I never heard tell of a pirate by the name of Huck Finn.

Tom. You kin be . . . Huck the Red-Handed, Joe can be Joe Harper, the Terror of the Seas, and I'll be Tom Sawyer, the Avenger of the Spanish Main. Where do we meet?

Huck.⎫
Joe. ⎭ *(With bated breath).* At the graveyard.

Tom. When?

Huck.⎫
Joe. ⎭ At midnight!

Tom. At midnight . . . exact.

(At this point there is a shout of 'Tom Sawyer!' from inside the house)

Tom. That's Aunt Polly. You'd better scat . . .

(Aunt Polly comes down the steps and through the garden, brandishing a switch in one hand and carrying, in the other, a half-eaten apple pie)

Aunt Polly. Where is that boy? I do swear I'll skin him . . . .

(She catches sight of Tom. Huck and Joe exit hurriedly)

Ah, Tom Sawyer. This time I really am goin' to do my duty by you. I thought you'd reformed, and then I find my apple pie . . . .

Tom. I haven't had it. Honest, Aunt!

Aunt Polly. . . . . eaten into, and I didn't put it out to cool not one hour ago. No—don't say another word. This time you ain't goin' to git away.

(Aunt Polly makes after Tom and, although he tries to evade her, she grabs him by the collar and marches him, still protesting, into the house)

Scene 2

(Just inside the graveyard. The outlines of tombstones can be seen in the background, while just left of stage-centre is a mound of earth. This is Hoss Williams's grave. The time is almost midnight. A shadow detaches itself from the general gloom and cautiously creeps in.)

Huck. Meow-w-w!

(There is no reply. He squats down and places his dead cat beside him.)

Lie there, old feller. Looks as though Tom's late.

(He begins to unpack a parcel he has brought with him. There is a faint 'meow-w' off-stage. **Huck** *gets to his feet.)*

That you, Tom?

Tom *(Coming in).* It's me, Huck.

Huck. Say, I'm sure glad you've turned up, Tom, I wus beginnin' to think you weren't comin'.

Tom *(Sitting down).* I had one or two things to atten' to, Huck. Look.

*(***Tom*** *holds up something on a chain)*

Huck. What is it?

Tom. It's Aunt Polly's watch. I crept into her room an' borrowed it. Now we'll know when it's midnight exact.

Huck. What time is it now?

Tom. I reckon it's five minutes to, near enough. *(He takes a packet from his pocket)* I brought some food. Aunt Polly whacked me fer hookin' that apple pie I never set eyes on, so she can't blame me fer takin' the rest. What you got, Huck?

Huck. I got some fried eggs, an' half a meat pie, an a whole piece of cheese an' a shinbone with considerable meat on it . . . .

Tom. Say, where d'you get them, Huck?

Huck. I dug 'em out the barrel where they throw their scraps at the hotel. I reckoned there'd be considerable good eatin' in it. *(He wipes the shinbone on his sleeve)* I had trouble gettin' this. There was a yeller mongrel after it, too. Take a bite?

*(***Huck*** *offers* **Tom** *the shinbone)*

Tom. No, thankee, Huck. I think I'll stick to the apple pie.

Huck *(After chewing for a moment at the shinbone).* I say, Tom. D'you believe dead people like it for us to be here?

Tom. I wish I knowed. It's awful solemn like, ain't it?

Huck. You bet it is.

Tom. Say, Huck. D'you reckin Hoss Williams kin hear us talkin'?

Huck. Course he does. Leastways, his spirit does.

Tom. I wish I'd said 'Mister' Williams. Sounds more respectful. But everybody calls him 'Hoss'.

Huck. A body can't be too careful how they talk 'bout these 'ere dead people, Tom.

Tom *(After a pause).* Huck, I just thought of somethin'!

Huck *(Finishing off the shinbone).* Uuh, uh?

Tom. That's . . . his grave right behind us.

Huck. That's right.

Tom. Suppose . . . suppose he were to stick his head up an' . . . say somethin'!

Huck. Oh, don't, Tom! I'm skeered. If I were to hear a noise from that there grave I reckin I wouldn't stop runnin' 'til I reached the Illinois!

Tom *(Looking at his watch).* It's comin' up to twelve, Huck . . . . Where are you goin'?

*(**Huck** has scrambled to his feet)*

Huck. I reckin it weren't such a good idea after all, Tom. There're easier ways to cure warts than hobnobbin' with devils. Joe was right . . . .

Tom. What about the treasure? You ain't goin' afore we've had a chance to look fer that?

Huck. You kin keep the treasure, Tom. That's if you kin find it. I'll just light out of here . . . .'

*(**Huck** is picking up his cat when **Tom** clutches him by the arm)*

Tom. Look!

*(**Tom** points off-stage)*

Huck. It's devil fire! It's devils, sure enough. We're goners.

Tom. Don't be afeard, I don't believe they'll bother us. We ain't doin' no harm.

Huck. We got to hide.

Tom. Quick! Down here behind this 'ere gravestone.

(Tom pulls Huck into concealment)

Huck. Lordy, Tom, I'm all of a shiver! Can you pray?

Tom. I'll try. 'Now I lay me down to sleep, I . . . .'

Huck. Sssh!

Tom. What is it, Huck?

Huck. They ain't devils!

Tom. No?

Huck. They're humans. One of 'em is, anyway. Listen! That's old Muff Potter's voice.

Tom. No, it ain't so.

Huck. I bet I know it. Don't you stir or budge. He ain't sharp enough to notice us. He's likely drunk, same as usual . . . .

Tom. Say, Huck, I know another o' them voices. It's . . . it's Injun Joe!

Huck. You sure, Tom?

Tom. Sure I'm sure. Look! You kin see their faces now—they're carryin' a red lantern. That's what you mistook fer the devil fire! ·

Huck. If it's Injun Joe I'd druther they was devils a dern sight! The murderin' half-breed. What kin they be up to?

Tom. Quiet! Git back in the shadows.

(Tom and Huck cringe back in the shadow of the gravestone)

Voice *(Off-stage).* Come on. This is the way.

Second Voice. I think we're off the track.

Voice. I tell you it's dead ahead. I kin see the grave.

(Injun Joe, Muff Potter and Dr Robinson come in. Muff Potter is pushing a wheelbarrow which contains a spade, a pick and a length of rope.)

Injun Joe. What did I tell you? Here's the grave.

Dr Robinson *(Taking out spade and pick from the wheelbarrow).* Let's not waste any time, then. You take the spade, and Muff can have the pick.

Injun Joe. Take the lantern, then.

*(*Injun Joe *gives* Dr Robinson *the lantern, and he and* Muff *clamber over the mound and begin to open the 'grave')*

Dr Robinson. Hurry, men. The moon looks as if she might come out any moment.

Muff *(Puffing under the exertion).* I reckin' it's a good thing they don't bury these paupers deep, eh, Injun Joe?

Injun Joe. Quit talkin' and swing that pick!

*(*Injun Joe *and* Muff *continue for a little longer)*

Muff. We're through! I kin feel the lid.

*(*Injun Joe *and* Muff *both put down their tools and scrape away the remaining earth)*

Give me a hand with the lid.

(They lift off the lid, then bend over and lift out the 'body' draped in white)

Give a hand, Doc!

*(*Dr Robinson *helps them to lift the body into the wheelbarrow)*

Dr Robinson *(Wiping his forehead).* Right. Now let's get out of here.

Injun Joe. Just a minute, sawbones. The cussed thing's here, and he'll stay here until you fork out another five dollars.

Muff. That's the talk, Joe!

Dr Robinson. Look here, Injun Joe. What's this mean? You wanted your pay in advance and I've paid you.

Injun Joe. Yes, and you done more than that. Five years ago you drove me away from your father's kitchen when I come to ask for something to eat, and said I warn't there for any good. When I swore I'd get even with you if it took a hundred years, your father had me jailed for a vagrant. D'you think I've forgot? The Indian blood ain't in me for nothin'! Now I've got you and you've got to settle.

Dr Robinson. You'll move that body. I'll not pay you a penny more.

Injun Joe. That big talk don't scare me none, Doc. You'll fork out five dollars or he stays right here! When folks find the body they'll know you robbed a grave for study . . . .

*(*Dr Robinson *suddenly strikes out and stretches* Injun Joe *on*

20

the ground)

Muff. Here, now! Don't you hit my pard!

(Muff leaps at Dr Robinson and they wrestle.
Injun Joe gets to his feet. He sees Muff Potter's knife, which he dropped when he attacked Dr Robinson, lying on the ground. He snatches it up and prowls round the other two, waiting his opportunity. Dr Robinson flings himself free, snatches up a short piece of plank from the coffin lid, and fells Muff to the ground with it. As Dr Robinson staggers back, Injun Joe stabs him from behind. Dr Robinson crumples to the ground.)

Injun Joe. That score is settled, damn you!

(Swiftly Injun Joe robs the body, taking the Doctor's wallet and putting it into his own pocket. Then he puts the knife in Muff Potter's hand, closing his fingers over the handle. Muff groans and moves, then sits up. He sees Dr Robinson, and then the knife in his hand.)

Muff. What's this, Joe?

(Muff holds his head)

Injun Joe. It's a dirty business. Why did you do it?

Muff. He's . . . he's dead? *(Injun Joe nods)* I . . . I didn't do it!

Injun Joe. Look here. That kind of talk won't wash! That's your knife, ain't it?

Muff. I can't recollect a thing. Tell me—honest, Joe—did I do it? I never meant to. 'Pon my soul an' honour, I never meant to, Joe. An' him so young an' promisin'! Tell me how it happened.

Injun Joe. Why, you two were scuffling, and he clouted you one with the headboard, and then up you come, all reelin' and staggerin' and out with your knife . . .

Muff *(Groaning and covering his face with his hands).* Oh, no Joe! No!

Injun Joe. . . . . and jammed it into him as he fetched you another awful clip, and here you've laid, dead as a wedge, 'til now.

Muff. I didn't know what I was doin'! I wish I may die this minute if I did. I never used a weapon in my life before, Joe. Everyone'll bear me out.

21

(He clutches at **Injun Joe's** *arm)*

Joe, don't tell! I always stood up for you, even when the whole town was against you. Don't you remember? Promise me you won't tell, Joe?

Injun Joe. No, you've always been fair an' square with me, Muff. I won't tell on you.

Muff. I'll bless you fer this the longest day I live! You're an angel, Joe. A real angel!

Injun Joe. This ain't any time fer blubberin'. We've got to get clear of this. You go that way, clear of the town and make your way down river. I'll go this way. Move, now, an' don't leave any tracks behind you.

Muff. Bless you, Joe! Bless you!

*(**Muff** stumbles off)*

Injun Joe *(Watching him go).* The old fool!

(He picks up the knife and turns it over in his hand)

He's so fuddled with the rum he'll keep on runnin' without givin' a thought to the knife. When he does think of it he'll be too skeered to cut back for it by himself—checken heart! *(He places the knife by the body)* That'll fix him!

*(**Injun Joe** then leaves. After a pause, **Tom** and **Huck** crawl out from behind the gravestone and approach the body. They are shivering with fright.)*

Tom. Huck, what d'you reckin'll come of this?

Huck. If the Doctor's dead, I reckin' hangin'll come of it.

Tom. He's dead all right, Huck!

Huck. Then I reckin' Muff'll hang. If they ketch him.

Tom. But Muff didn't do it, Hucky!

Huck. I know it, Tom.

Tom. Who'll tell? We?

Huck. What are you talkin' about? Suppose we tell and Injun Joe don't hang? Why, he'd kill us dead if it's the last thing he did!

22

Tom. That's just what I was thinkin', Huck.

Huck. If anyone tells, it ought to be Muff Potter.

Tom. But Muff Potter thinks he did it himself, Huck. You were right here with me. You saw Injun Joe double-cross him. He put the knife right into his hand.

Huck. You're right, Tom.

Tom. Huck, you sure we kin keep mum?

Huck. We ain't got no choice, Tom. That Injun devil wouldn't think any more of drownin' us than a couple of cats if we was to squeak 'bout this and he 'scaped hangin'! Look, Tom, let's take an' swear to each other—that's what we got to do—swear to keep mum!

Tom. I'm agreed. We'll hold hands an' swear . . . .

Huck. Oh, no, that wouldn't do fer this. There ought to be writin' about this—and blood!

Tom. I'll write us an oath. *(He fishes a piece of paper from his pocket and a stub of a pencil)* Now, if you kin just prick your finger, Huck, and get us some blood I'll have this ready in no time.

Huck *(Taking a pin from his hat).* Right, Tom. *(He pricks his finger and squeezes a drop of blood)* Ouch!

Tom *(After a moment).* It's finished! Listen. *(He reads)* 'Huck Finn and Tom Sawyer swears they will keep mum about this and they wish they may drop down dead in their tracks if they ever tell and rot.' Now, give me the pin.

*(He takes the pin and signs his name in blood from **Huck**'s finger. Then **Huck** takes the pin and does the same.)*

There! It's finished! Now we'll put it under this rock . . . .

*(**Tom** bends down and hides the note)*

Huck. Tom, does this keep us from ever tellin'—always?

Tom. Course it does! It don't make any difference what happens, we got to keep mum. If we don't we'll drop down dead! Don't you know that?

Huck. I reckin so.

(There is the sound of a dog howling, loud and mournful, from

23

beyond the graveyard. **Tom** *and* **Huck** *clasp each other in an agony of fright.)*

Huck. Oh, Tom, we're done for! A stray dog howlin' at midnight means certain death for them as hears it.

(The dog howls again)

Tom. I reckin we're both done for, Huck! We're goners. There ain't no mistake where I'll go. I been so wicked. I might have been good, like Sid—but no, I wouldn't. If ever I get off this time I'll just *waller* in Sunday-Schools!

Huck. You think *you're* bad? Confound it, you're just old pie 'longside what I am! Oh, Lordy, Lordy, Lordy, I wisht I only had half your chance!

Tom *(Snatching up his parcel—or what remains of it).* I'm gettin' out of here! And I ain't goin' to stop runnin' 'til mornin'!

(He dashes out)

Huck *(Starting after him, then rushing back for the remains of his shinbone).* Hey! Wait fer me, Tom Sawyer! Wait fer me!

Scene 3

(The graveyard again the following afternoon. A crowd of men, women and children are looking at the footmarks in the ground. Then another group enters the graveyard—there are about a dozen people in this group, with, perhaps, some more off-stage. In the centre is the **Sheriff,** *leading* **Muff Potter** *by the arm and* **Judge Thatcher** *is nearby.* **Injun Joe** *is close behind.* **Aunt Polly** *and* **Sid** *are at the rear of the crowd.* **Tom** *and* **Huck** *creep on as inconspicuously as possible. The crowd is in an ugly, excitable mood.)*

Sheriff. Stand up! We've brought you here to answer a few questions.

Crowd. That's right! Make him answer, Sheriff!

First Woman. Look at him! He's so scared he can't hardly stand! That's a sure sign of guilt!

Crowd. He's guilty!

24

Muff *(Trembling)*. I'm doin' the best I kin. My knees won't hold me right! *(He looks at* **Injun Joe**) Oh, Injun Joe, you promised me you'd never tell!

First Man. D'you hear that?

Second Man. Yes, we all heard it!

Sheriff. Quiet! *(Silence ensues)* Is this your knife?

(The **Sheriff** *shows* **Muff** *his knife)*

Third Man. Course it's his, Sheriff! Everyone in the town knows it!

Sheriff. Is it your knife?

Muff *(Faintly)*. Somethin' told me if I didn't come back an' get it . . . tell 'em, Joe. Tell 'em. It ain't any use any more!

Sheriff. You heard him. Tell!

Injun Joe. It was like this. Him and the doctor got to arguin', an' the Doc struck out sudden, and next moment they were grapplin' an' tramplin' the ground. There, you kin see it yet . . . .

(The **Crowd** *surges round to look)*

Sheriff. Keep back there! Go on.

Injun Joe. Then the doctor he snatched up a board and fetched him one, an' he fell down flat. Then up he comes, reelin' an' staggerin'. He outs with his knife an' jammed it into the doctor an' was off like a streak.

(The **Crowd** *murmurs ominously)*

Sheriff. You heard that, Muff Potter. Now speak! Is that story true?

*(**Muff** tries to speak but the words won't come. He moistens his lips and nods. The* **Crowd** *breaks loose and moves towards him. Someone cries* 'Get him'.)

Sheriff. Leave the prisoner alone! Order!

Fourth Man. We'll take care of him fer you, Sheriff! *(He grabs at* **Muff**. *Several other men grab his arms)* We know how to treat murderers!

Judge Thatcher. You heard the Sheriff! Take your hands off that man!

(Slowly they do as he tells them)

We'll have no mob rule here! This is a law-abiding town. If he's guilty he'll be punished, but only after a fair and open trial.

Fifth Man. I reckin the Judge's right.

Second Woman. O' course he's right, you great blockhead!

Sheriff. Make way, there . . . . *(The* **Crowd** *parts)* Come along!

> *(The* **Sheriff** *leads* **Muff Potter** *away, followed by* **Injun Joe** *and the greater part of the crowd.* **Tom** *and* **Huck** *hang behind.* **Aunt Polly** *is about to depart with* **Sid,** *when she notices them.)*

Aunt Polly. Why, Tom, come along home! What d'you want to hang around here for?

Tom. I . . . I'm comin', Aunt Polly.

Aunt Polly. Why, child, I do declare you're sick! You're as white as a ghost!

Tom. I'm fine, Aunt.

Sid. He was pitchin' around in his sleep an' talkin' so much he kept me awake about half the night.

Aunt Polly. That's a bad sign. What you got on your mind, Tom?

Sid. He said: 'It's blood, it's blood, that's what it is!' He said that over an' over! An' then he said: 'Don't torment me so—I'll tell.'

Aunt Polly. Tell what? What is it you'll tell, Tom?

Tom. Nothin', Aunt Polly . . . nothin' at all.

Aunt Polly. I reckin' the trouble is them doughnuts you ate. Wait 'til I get you home. I'll give you a dose o' black treacle an' molasses. Come along, Sidney.

> *(She leaves with* **Sid***)*

Joe Harper *(Rushing in and almost colliding with* **Aunt Polly***).* Sorry, Miss Sawyer! *(To* **Tom** *and* **Huck***)* Hi, fellers!

Tom. Hi, Joe.

Huck. Hi.

Joe. I sneaked back. Say, ain't it excitin'? D'you reckon they'll hang Muff? That crowd was in a pretty ugly mood.

Tom. I reckin it was.

Joe. An' did you notice Injun Joe glarin' at you, Tom? When you made a move to help Muff—that time he almost fell down? He looked as though he'd like to kill you!

Tom. Do you mean it?

Joe. An' he kept lookin' at you every now an' then after that. I'd be scared to meet him on the street, Tom, if I was you!

Tom. Shucks. Injun Joe ain't nothin'! I ain't scared of him!

Joe. I bet he is. Don't you think so, Hucky?

Huck. I reckin so. I reckin he's track down anybody he's set out to get.

Tom. Oh, don't Huck! Don't let's talk about it!

Joe. Say, when are we goin' to turn pirates? I'm gettin' tired of waitin'. You said you'd go.

Tom }
Huck } *(To each other).* Geewhillikins! The raft!

Tom. I'd clean forgotten 'bout the raft!

Huck. If we work on it we kin have it ready fer tonight!

Tom. We'll do it.

Joe. That's bully!

Tom. We'll have to borrow some tools—a pick an' a shovel, maybe— an' snake some food from home the way we said.

Huck. We kin spend the afternoon workin' on the raft . . . .

Joe. An' then go home fer tea an' to collect the booty . . . .

Huck. What's booty?

Joe. Why, booty's what pirate's have. It's . . . ain't that so, Tom?

Tom. Sure. Provisions an' food an' things they hook. They capture it an' then they take it to their island or their cave.

Joe. Then that's settled. We'll meet when the moon comes up!

Tom. }
Huck. } When the moon comes up!

(They go off)

27

ACT TWO

Scene 1

(Jackson's Island, about six o'clock the following day. A small clearing surrounded by trees. In the background are the ruins of an old house—crumbling, overgrown with weeds. Only two walls remain standing, and an old fireplace.

Tom, Huck and Joe are sprawling round a camp fire. They have just finished supper.)

Joe. Ain't it jolly?

Tom. It's the best!

Joe. What would the boys say if they could see us?

Tom. Say? Why, they'd just die to be here—hey, Hucky?

Huck. I reckin so. Anyways, I'm suited. I don't want nothin' better'n this. I don't ever get enough to eat gen'ally.

Tom *(Offering him the frying-pan).* Have another piece o' bacon, Huck. Go on, it's the last.

Huck. Thanks, Tom. *(Huck takes it)* Sure you don't want a share?

Tom. I reckin I'll jest clean my teeth on this here green apple.

(Tom takes an apple from his pocket)

Joe. You'll git stomach ache an' bad dreams from green apples, my mother alus says.

Tom *(Scornfully).* Pirates don't git stomach ache, Joe Harper! Seems to me you ain't decided whether you're a genwine pirate yet.

Joe. I am that! I am a genwine pirate! Anyways, if you eats green apples you git bad dreams—pirate or not! *(Pause)* Tell us what pirates do, Tom.

Tom. I've told you once.

Joe. I know, but tell us agin.

Tom. Well, they jest have a bully time—take ships an' burn 'em, an' get money an' bury it in awful places in their island where there's ghosts an' things to watch it, an' kill everybody in the ships an' make them walk the plank . . . .

Joe. An' don't they wear the bulliest clothes! An' gold an' silver an' diamonds!

Huck. Who?

Joe. Why, the pirates.

Huck *(Looking at his own clothes).* Then I reckin I ain't fitted to be a pirate. I ain't got none but these.

Tom. That ain't no account, Huck.

Huck. Ain't it, Tom?

Tom. Course it ain't! All pirates start out poor—leastways, those I've heard about ain't had nothin' more'n a pair o' trousers an' a shirt when they made a start. They get their silks an' satins an' jewels an' such-like from the ships they take.

Huck. Honest injun, Tom?

Tom. Sure, Huck! Why, as soon as we take a ship we'll have all three of us rigged out like . . . like three o' them old European kings. Like I said—all silks an' satins an' scented like a skunk in Spring!

Huck. Scent?

Tom. Sure, Huck. Y'see, they never washed 'cept when it was their birthday or when they had a coronation or somethin' special, so they just had to use scent or folks wouldn't hev bin able to stand near 'em.

Huck. I reckin that's all right, then.

Joe *(Getting to his feet).* I'll just fetch some more wood. The fire's gettin' low.

Tom *(Alert).* Jest a minute!

Joe. What is it?

Tom. Listen! I thought I heard . . . *(There is silence as all three boys* *listen intently, then a dull, muffled boom is heard)*

There it is!

Huck. What is it?

Tom. It's the cannon!

Joe. What cannon?

Tom. The cannon they alus fire from the ferry-boat when someone's drownded! Come on—we kin see the river from up here!

(He rushes a slight 'bank' at the back of the stage, followed by **Joe** *and* **Huck***)*

Joe *(Pointing).* There it is! It's the old *Savannah.*

Tom. Ain't she jest crowded with people! I reckin half the town must be on board.

Huck. An' look at those skiffs an' row boats! One, two, three, four . . . . I reckin there must be close on a score on 'em!

(There is another muffled 'boom')

Tom. There she goes agin! Did you see that, Joe? Did you see the smoke?

Joe. They done that last summer when Bill Turner got drownded. They shoot a cannon over the water, an' that makes him come to the top. Yes, an' they take loaves of bread an' put quicksilver in 'em an' set 'em afloat, and wherever there's anybody that's drownded they'll float right there an' stop!

Huck. By jingo, I wish I was over there now!

Joe. So do I. I'd give heaps to know who it is!

(They continue craning their necks)

Joe. Look! Ain't that the sheriff in that boat with the minister? And I'm sure . . . .

Tom. Boys! I know who's drownded! It's US!

*(***Huck** *and* **Joe** *look at* **Tom**, *open-mouthed, for a moment. Then realisation dawns.)*

Joe. Whoopee!

Huck. We're drownded!

Tom. We're dead! We're famous!

All. We're drownded!

(They cheer, and join hands and do a wild jig around the fire. In the middle of it **Tom** *breaks off and raises a finger.)*

Tom. Whist!

(They all listen intently. A voice is heard, clear and distinct, but some distance away.)

Voice. This way girls! Keep to the path!

Tom. Gosh!

Joe. It's the MASTER!

Tom. He's after us! *(He is suddenly galvanised into action)* Quick! the fire! *(He kicks soil over it)* Get rid of those sticks, Joe! An' Huck—hide that fryin' pan!

Joe *(Picking up the firewood).* Oh, Lordy, Lordy, we're for it, Tom . . . .

Tom. Quit talkin' and start movin'! If he finds us he'll flay the hide off'n us . . . .

Joe *(With an armful of sticks).* I know that, Tom, I know that! What shall we do?

Tom. Scatter, that's what we'll do! Scatter an' hide 'til he goes by.

Joe. He'll smell us out! I reckin . . . ooohh!

(The voice is heard again—this time much nearer)

Voice. This way! I think I can detect a clearing ahead. Keep to the path.

Tom. SCATTER!

(The boys dive for cover. **Huck** *hides behind a tree,* **Joe** *conceals himself behind a ruined wall, and* **Tom** *ducks behind the window. The* **Schoolmaster,** *a stern, forbidding figure in black, carrying a short switch, enters. He is followed by three girls—***Becky Thatcher,** **Amy Lawrence** *and* **Josie Preston.** *)*

Schoolmaster. Come along girls! Don't loiter. Pick up your feet. Try to behave like ladies even though you're on a nature ramble.

Amy. Oh, Mr Snodgrass, my feet are aching so! Can't we just rest a minute?

Josie. Please, Mr Snodgrass, I declare I've got a wart on my ankle as big as a loganberry!

(Josie stands on one foot and rubs her ankle)

Schoolmaster *(Looking back).* Where have the boys got to? If they've slipped off behind my back . . . ! *(He gives the switch a vigorous swish)* We'll rest for a minute to give them a chance to catch up.

(The girls sit down on stumps, etc.)

Josie. I think the boys have slipped off, Mr Snodgrass. I heard Jesse Morgan sayin' to Mike Dolan that it weren't right that they should be trampin' round lookin' fer ol' leaves and caterpillars when they could be draggin' the river for them poor, drowned boys! That's what he said—cut my throat an' hope to die!

(Becky, who is sitting on a dead tree stump, suddenly bursts into a loud wailing)

Becky. Boooohh!! He . . . he's . . . dead, an' I'll . . . never . . . see him again! *(She dabs her face with her handkerchief)*

Schoolmaster. Nonsense, Becky! Dry your eyes and stop snivelling like a workhouse child. No one's dead.

Becky *(Still tearful).* But . . . but . . . Mr S . . . Snodgrass, they . . . they're dragging the . . . the river! And why should they do that if . . . if no . . . no one's . . . drowned? Awwh!

(Becky bursts into tears again)

Amy. Becky's right! They're all drowned—the three of them! Tom an' . . . an' Joe, and Huck Finn! An' we'll never . . . see any of them again! Booohh!!

(Amy too bursts into tears)

Schoolmaster. Will you be SILENT!

(They stop crying aloud, although they still snivel into their handkerchiefs)

Just because a few foolish folk lose their heads is no reason for us to do the same.

Becky. But Mr Sno . . . Snodgrass, poor Tom . . . .

Amy. And . . . poor Joe!

Schoolmaster. Poor Tom and poor Joe are no doubt laughing up their sleeves at all the fuss and commotion they've caused. It wouldn't surprise me if they were on this very island . . . . *(He looks suspiciously round.* **Tom** *and* **Joe** *duck their heads hurriedly.)*

They've played truant and they're too scared to return and face the consequences! Sooner or later they'll have to return and then . . . *(He gives another vigorous swish of the switch)* then there will be weeping and wailing and gnashing of teeth!

Amy *(Breaking into a fresh wail of anguish).* Poor Tom!

Schoolmaster. Will you cease this miserable cauterwauling at once? At once, do you hear, Amy Lawrence? If there is one thing I detest . . . . *(He suddenly stiffens)* Quiet! Don't *move! (He picks up his butterfly net)* Who would have thought it! Here in this . . . quietly . . . quietly!

(The **Schoolmaster** *extends his net and moves, crab-wise, across the stage. As he raises the net to capture the 'butterfly'* **Becky** *breaks out again.)*

Becky. Aaaahh! He's drowned! I know he's . . . drooowned!

Schoolmaster *(Whirling round in a fierce temper).* Ah! He's gone! You stupid, snivelling, little GIRL! But I'll catch him. Yes, I'll get him if it takes me all day! Stay here—don't move from this spot until I return . . . .

Becky.⎫
Amy. ⎬ Aaaaahh!!

Schoolmaster. And for Heaven's sake BLOW YOUR NOSE!

(The **Schoolmaster** *dashes off, butterfly net raised. The girls remain seated on their respective stumps, etc.* **Becky** *and* **Amy** *are still sniffing into their handkerchiefs.* **Josie Preston,** *however, is quite composed. She sits upright with her hands in her lap, looking scornfully at the other two.)*

Josie *(In a bored voice).* I do declare, I've not heard such snivellin' and snufflin' since I was in Second Grade—and that's a fact!

Becky. It . . . it's all right . . . for you, Josie Preston. Tom never meant anythin' to you!

Amy. Neether did . . . poor Joe! An' now he's dead!

Becky. They're *both* dead!

Amy.
Becky. } Booohh!!

Josie. I should certainly think they didn't. *(She draws herself up primly)* I have better things to do with my time than play around with dirty little boys . . . .

Becky *(Hotly)*. Tom warn't dirty—at least, not on Sundays. And he gave me wonderful presents. Once he gave me a whole glass doorknob—genwine glass—and another time he taught me to draw, an' . . . an' he was good an' kind . . . and you're only jealous 'cause he wouldn't look at you!

Josie. That's not true!

Becky. It is true! It is! Ain't I right, Amy?

Amy. Course you're right, Becky. Josie's only jealous 'cause no boy'll look at her.

Josie. They will, they will! Why, Tom came to my birthday party and so did Joe.

Amy. Yes, only because your mother baked a chocolate cake!

Josie. Wasn't so!

Amy. It was so! So there!

Josie. It wasn't, it wasn't, it wasn't! *(She starts to cry)* Oh, I hate you, I hate you!

Becky. You've got freckles an' knock knees, an' sticky-out teeth . . . ooh!

(Josie jumps off her log and hits her)

Josie. Don't you call me names, Becky Thatcher! You're a liar!

Becky. An' you're another!

Josie. Oh, I'm not going to stay here. I'm going home to my mother. I'll tell her what you called me!

(Josie runs off)

Becky. And I'll tell my father! And my father's a judge and he'll put your father in gaol, and then where'll you be—little Miss Smartypants!

(Becky sticks out her tongue at Josie)

Amy. Do you think Mr Snodgrass was right, Becky? 'Bout Tom and Joe, I mean? Do you think they're just playin' hookey from school?

Becky. I don't know, Amy. I 'spect so. Tom can swim almost like a fish.

Amy. Joe can swim like a fish, too.

Becky. But not as good as Tom. Tom can swim better'n any boy in St Petersburg.

Amy. Tom's a good swimmer, I know, but Joe's a better.

Becky *(A little annoyed)*. I know Tom better'n you, Amy. We're engaged.

Amy. Oh, poohy! We was engaged *years* ago! *(Airily)* I got tired of him.

Becky. You're just talkin' through a hole in your head, Amy Lawrence. You're hardly no better than that silly Josie Preston!

Amy. If that's the way you're goin' to talk, Becky Thatcher, then I'm going!

Becky. I won't mind!

Amy. Very well then—I will go!

(Amy jumps up and stalks away)

Becky. Amy! Don't . . . I didn't mean . . .

(Becky looks around her. During the previous scene it has been getting steadily darker. She settles down nervously and looks around again. Suddenly, an owl hoots in the gathering twilight, startling her.)

Amy! Amy! Wait for me!

(Becky dashes away. After a moment the boys emerge from their respective hiding places.)

Joe. I thought they was never goin' away, Tom. It was a good idea of yours to do that owl-call.

Tom. I reckin it was at that.

Joe. Say, did you hear old Snodgrass say what he was goin' to do to us? He sounded awful mean.

Tom. That's just one more reason why we got to keep on bein' pirates,

Joe. If we went back to school now we'd be skinned alive fer sure! What you lookin' fer, Huck?

Huck *(On his hands and knees)*. I'm lookin' fer a spark o' fire fer my pipe. Ah! here she is!

(Huck puts his head to the ground and blows vigorously)

Dang it! She's gone out—an' I was lookin' forward to a smoke, too!

Tom *(Taking a box from his pocket)*. Here, I've got a box of them new-fangled lucifer matches. Try one, Huck.

(Huck takes the matches. They all sit round the remains of the fire. Huck strikes a match and lights his pipe, watched by the other two.)

Huck *(Puffing away)*. Thet's better! I nivver feel right without I have my pipe after supper! When I hev any supper, that is.

Tom *(Enviously)*. I wish you'd let me have a go, Huck.

Huck. Sure, Tom. *(He hands him the pipe)* Draw nice an' steady now.

Tom. Thanks, Huck. *(He puffs)* Say, this is dandy! Why, it's just easy! If I'd known *this* was all, I'd a learnt long ago!

Joe. Let me try, Tom.

(Tom hands him the pipe)

Huck. Keep her drawin' strong, Joe.

(Joe puffs away determinedly)

Tom. Why, many a time I've looked at people smokin' and thought, 'Well, I wish I could do that,' but I never thought I could. You've heard me talk just that way, haven't you Huck?

Huck *(Who has lit a second pipe)*. Yes, heaps of times.

Tom. Once down there by the slaughter house. Bob Tanner was there, an' Johnny Miller, an' Jeff Thatcher. Don't you remember, Huck, me sayin' that?

Huck. Yes, that's so. That's the day after I lost a white alley—no, the day before.

Tom. There, Huck r'collects it.

Joe. I b'lieve I could smoke this pipe all day. I don't feel sick.

Tom. Here, it's my turn!

(Joe hands over the pipe)

Huck. Try this here, Joe.

(Huck hands him his second pipe)

Tom. I could smoke this all day, too. I bet Jeff Thatcher couldn't.

Joe. Jeff Thatcher! Why, he'd keel over with just two draws! So would Johnny Miller.

Tom. Johnny Miller! I'd like to see him tackle it jest once.

(They both puff contentedly for a moment)

Joe. I wish the boys could see us now.

Tom. Say, don't say anythin' 'bout this, and sometime when they're around I'll come up to you an' say, kind o' casual, 'Joe, got a pipe?' And you'll say, careless like, you'll say: 'Yes. I got my old pipe, but my tobacker ain't very good.' And I'll say: 'Oh, that's all right, if it's strong enough.' And then you'll out with your pipes and we'll light up, and then just see 'em look!

*(The boys burst into uproarious laughter. An agonised look comes over **Joe's** face, and he rises to his feet.)*

Tom. Where you off to?

Joe *(Faintly, clutching his stomach).* I . . . reckin I'd better fetch some more . . . firewood.

(He stumbles off)

Tom *(Calling after him).* But there ain't no fire!

(He shrugs, and sits down again. After a few moments he, too, rises to his feet.)

'Scuse me, Huck!

*(**Tom** stumbles off after **Joe**. **Huck** chuckles to himself, and knocks out the pipes. He stretches out, then raises himself on one elbow and picks up something on one finger.)*

Huck. Hello, ma'am! I guess I almost flattened them. If I were you I wouldn't hang around here. It ain't safe . . .

*(**Huck** lifts his arm)*

'Lady-bug, lady-bug, fly away home,
Your house is on fire, your children's alone!'

(Tom and Joe come back, both looking sheepish and rather white-faced)

Huck. I should have warned you. That tobacker's strong if you ain't used to it.

Joe *(Still faintly)*. I think I'll go to bed.

Huck. I think it's time we all turned in.

(They settle down in a rough circle)

Huck. Goo'night Tom, Joe.

Joe. 'Night.

Tom. G'night, Huck.

(Within a few seconds they are all asleep. An owl hoots in the trees. There is the sound of a fox barking in the far distance. Tom tosses restlessly. From somewhere on the other side of the stage, which is in darkness, there comes, very faintly, the sound of a woman sobbing. Tom begins to murmur in his sleep. The weeping becomes louder, and then slowly, the far side of the stage lightens to reveal Aunt Polly and Mrs Harper sitting side by side. Mrs Harper is weeping, and Aunt Polly is trying to comfort her)

Aunt Polly. There now, Mrs Harper, don't cry! Don't take on so!

Mrs Harper. I can't help it, Miss Sawyer, I jest can't help it! An' they were so young, too. . . . *(She sobs)* They weren't bad—jest mischievous . . . .

Aunt Polly. Tom was jest giddy an' harum-scarum. He warn't any more responsible than a colt. He never meant any harm, and he was the best-hearted that ever was.

Mrs Harper. It was jest so with my Joe—always full of his devilment, and up to every kind of mischief, but he was jest as unselfish and kind as he could be! And to think I went and whipped him for takin' that cream, never once thinkin' that I throwed it out myself 'cause it was sour. And I'll never see him again in this world, never, never, never, poor abused boy!

(She sobs again)

Only last week he bursted a shootin' cracker right under my nose, and I knocked him sprawlin'! Oh, if it was to do over again I'd hug an' bless him for it.

Aunt Polly. Yes, yes, yes. I know jest how you feel, Mrs Harper. I know exactly how you feel. Only yesterday noon, my Tom took an' filled the cat's milk full of weed killer, and I did think the poor creature would tear the house down! And God forgive me, I cracked Tom's head with my thimble, poor boy, poor dead boy!

Mrs Harper. Oh, I don't know how to give him up, I don't know how to give him up! He was such a comfort to me, though he tormented my heart out of me almost!

Aunt Polly. There, we must try to be patient. 'The Lord giveth, and the Lord taketh away. Blessed be the name of the Lord.'

(**Aunt Polly**'s *voice fades out with the last words, and at the same time the light fades.* **Tom**, *who has been tossing more and more restlessly, shouts out in his sleep.*)

Tom. I'm sorry, Aunt Polly, I'm sorry! I ain't really dead!

(*He staggers to his feet, stumbling over the sleeping* **Huck**)

It's me, Aunt Polly! Tom! I'm a comin' home. I'm sorry I grieved you . . . I'm sorry!

Huck (*Waking up*). Hey! What's a goin' on here? What you roamin' about fer, Tom?

Tom (*Still half-asleep*). I . . . I thought I heard voices.

Huck. Voices? Whose voices?

Tom. I . . . don't rightly know, Huck. It sounded like Aunt Polly's.

Joe (*Waking up*). What you two talkin' about in the middle of the night? I want to git some sleep.

Huck. I guess Tom's been dreamin'. He's been hearin' voices.

Joe. I told you you'd git bad dreams if you ate green apples.

Tom. I ain't been dreamin'! I tell you I heard voices!

Joe. What they say?

Tom. I can't rightly tell you. I thought I could hear Aunt Polly. . . .

Joe. Aunt Polly! That's proves you've been dreamin'! What would your

Aunt Polly be doin' out here on Jackson's Island?

Tom *(Reluctantly).* I guess you're right, Joe. . . .

Joe. Course I'm right! Come on, let's turn in again. I'm tired.

(Joe lies down once more. **Tom** *and* **Huck** *follow suit. Suddenly,* **Huck** *sits upright.)*

Huck. Listen!

Joe. Aw, what's the matter now? You hearin' voices too?

Huck *(Scrambling to his feet).* There's somethin' out there!

Tom *(Getting up).* Then I did hear voices! I wasn't dreamin'!

Huck. Look! Kin you see anythin', Tom?

Tom. It's kind o' dark an' shadowy, Huck . . . *(*Tom *clutches* Huck's *arm)* I kin see a lantern!

Huck. A . . . red lantern.

Tom. An' it's movin' this way!

Joe *(Joining them).* What's this about a lantern?

Tom *(Grabbing his pack from the ground).* Someone's headin' this way! Hide these things!

(He pushes it behind the wall)

Don't stand there, Joe. *Move!*

Joe. But who's comin'?

Tom. I don't know. But if it's who I think it is we'd better make ourselves scarce! Huck! *(He looks round)* Where's Huck?

Huck *(From behind the door of the ruined house where he scuttled as soon as he saw the lantern).* Here, Tom.

Tom *(Dragging* Joe *after him).* Come *on!*

(They disappear through the door and close it after them. Then it opens a fraction, and their heads are seen peering round it.)

Tom. Ssht!

Huck *(Hoarsely).* W . . . What is it?

Tom. Ssht! There! Hear it?

Joe. Oh my! Let's run!

Tom. Keep still! Don't you budge! They're coming right this way!

(Their heads disappear and the door closes. After a moment two mysterious figures enter. One is a rough-looking man with a beard. The other is muffled in a cloak; he is wearing a sombrero, bushy white whiskers and a pair of green spectacles. Both carry staffs, and the second man is clutching a small, canvas bag.)

First Man. No. I've thought it all over an' I don't like it. It's dangerous.

Injun Joe *(For it is* **Joe** *in disguise).* Dangerous? Milksop!

Thomson *(We'll call him this).* I still say it's too dangerous. I kin still feel those dogs bayin' at my heels.

Injun Joe. What's more dangerous than that job we did up yonder—but nothin's come of it?

Thomson. That's different. That was away up river, an' not another house about. 'Twon't ever be known we tried to break in, anyway, long as we didn't succeed.

Injun Joe. Well, what's more dangerous than us comin' up here in the daytime?

Thomson. I know—but there weren't any place as handy after that fool of a job. I tell you, I want to get out of here, Joe. . . .

Injun Joe. Don't call me Joe. I'm the Spaniard. Don't fergit it! Look, sit down. . . . *(They both sit down)* After we've rested you go back to the river where you belong. We'll do that dangerous job after I've spied around a little an' things look right fer it. Then we'll leg it fer Texas together. How's that sound to you?

Thomson. Why can't we leave fer Texas now? Never mind the other job. We've got six hundred dollars in silver. That ought to be enough.

Injun Joe. Not fer me it ain't. 'Sides, I can't skip out of town 'til Potter's trial's over tomorrow. I've got to give evidence. If I lit out now they'd suspect me and be after me. So, we stay.

Thomson. I still don't like it. . . .

Injun Joe. Stop complainin'. *(He gets to his feet)* We'd better find somewhere to bury the swag 'til we do the other job—somewhere good an' deep.

41

Thomson. What about that ruined fireplace? We could bury it under the grate.

Injun Joe. I reckin we could at that. *(They go over to the fireplace and kneel down)* Give me your knife.

*(**Thomson** hands him his knife; they begin to excavate a hole. The door behind them opens, and the frightened faces of the boys peer through.)*

Injun Joe. Hello!

Thomson. What is it?

Injun Joe. Half-rotten plank—no, it's a box. I b'lieve. Here, bear a hand, and we'll see what it's here for. Never mind—I've broke a hole! *(He puts in his hand, and draws out a handful of gold)* Man, it's money!

Thomson. Money?

Injun Joe. Gold! Solid, genwine gold!

Thomson. Let's have it out. *(They pull out an old, mouldering box)* Break open the lid.

*(**Injun Joe** breaks the lid open, and they stare in astonishment)*

Injun Joe. Pard, there's thousands of dollars here!

Thomson. 'Twas always said Murrel's gang hung out round here—this must be their booty.

Injun Joe. It looks like it.

Thomson. Now we won't need to do that job.

Injun Joe. You don't know me. 'Tain't robbery altogether—it's revenge. I'll need your help in it. When it's finished—then Texas. Go home to your Nance and kids and wait 'til you hear from me.

Thomson. Well, if you say so. . . . *(He breaks off)* What's that? *(He turns round, and the boys disappear behind the door)*

Injun Joe. What's what?

Thomson. I thought I heard somethin'. I guess I was mistaken. What'll we do with this? Bury it agin?

Injun Joe. Sure—and bury it deep!

(They replace the gold in the fireplace)
Now we'll put our silver dollars in, too.

(They place the bag in the hole, empty in the soil, and stamp hard upon it)

I reckin that ought to hold it.

Thomson. What now?

Injun Joe. As I said. You get off home and lie low 'til I come fer you. I'll slip back into town.

Thomson. What time's the trial?

Injun Joe. Eleven sharp.

Thomson. D'you think Muff Potter'll hang if they find him guilty?

Injun Joe. They'll find him guilty right enough, and he'll hang. The boy will see to that. Right, off you go. I'll give you a few minutes and then I'll leave myself by the other path. We don't want some early bird of a raft-hand to see us together.

Thomson. Right.

*(**Thomson** slinks off. **Injun Joe** stands looking after him, then he looks at the fireplace.)*

Injun Joe. There must be close on five thousand dollars there. *(He strokes his chin)* Too few to share.

*(**Injun Joe** looks around him, and then sets off in the same direction as **Thomson**. After a moment the door opens, and **Tom**, **Huck** and **Joe** step cautiously out. **Joe** is about to say something, but **Tom** puts his finger to his lips. They creep over to the fireplace, and in a few seconds have unearthed the box again. **Tom** throws back the lid and they stare open-mouthed.)*

Huck. Geewhillikins!

Joe *(Plunging his hand into the box).* Gold! Real gold!

Tom *(Letting the coins trickle through his fingers).* Real gold—an' it's all ours! I always said we'd get it. It's too good to believe, but we have got it fer sure!

Joe. We'll be rich. Real rich like them European kings!

Tom. We'll be richer! Why, they'll be small change compared to us.

Joe. What you goin' to do with your share, Tom?

Tom. I'm goin' to buy myself a drum an' a bull pup an' a red necktie an' . . . an' a few other things. And I'll buy Aunt Polly that crystal vase she's always wanted.

Joe. An' I'm goin' to get myself a real, genwine ten-dollar air rifle like Mike Dolan, only better'n his. And I'll buy my mother a red velvet dress and my father a box of cigars—perhaps even two boxes. What you goin' to buy with your share, Huck?

Huck. I'm going to buy myself three meals a day fer the rest o' my life—an' a pair of shoes. Real, leather shoes.

Tom. But you always said you could never abide shoes, Huck.

Huck. There was no point in wishin' after 'em. I hadn't any money then. Say, Tom, it ain't stealin' is it? They found it first.

Tom. Course it ain't stealin', Huck! I reckin it rightly belongs to whoever those old robbers stole it off, but since they're most likely dead it's ours.

Huck. You sure, Tom? I don't want any share in it if it ain't rightly mine.

Tom. Whoever finds one of these hidden treasures it's his. It says that in all the old books. You kin ask Judge Thatcher if you don't believe me.

Huck. Oh, I believe you, Tom.

Joe. Say, what about Injun Joe?

Tom. What about him?

Joe. He won't like it when he comes back an' finds it gone. He'll be real mad!

Tom. Let him be mad then. I'm not worryin' about Injun Joe.

Joe. But don't you see? He'll track it down. He'll find out who's taken it, an' then he'll . . . why, he'll kill us!

Huck. Joe, you don't mean it?

Tom. Never mind 'bout Injun Joe. What do we want to be afraid for? Look, we'll take the money an' divide it into three parts. We kin carry it inside our shirts and. . . . *(He stops)* Boys!

Joe. What is it?

Tom. I've jest had an idea. It's a bully idea!

Huck. Then tell us.

Tom. What day is it tomorrow?

Huck. It's Sunday.

Tom. Right. And tomorrow there's goin' to be a funeral.

Joe. A funeral?

Tom. Preachin' an' everythin'. For *us*. They think we're dead. Don't you see? They've searched the river an' they haven't found us so they'll think we're dead! I'll wager my share of the gold the Minister'll hold a funeral fer us. Aunt Polly'll be there, an' Mary an' Sid, an' your mother an' father, Joe, an' the Widow Douglas 'cause she was mighty fond of Huck. I'll allow half the town'll be there! Let's get into town early an' hide ourselves 'fore the service begins and listen to the Minister preach our funeral sermon.

Joe. Whoo-pee! That's an *idea*!

Tom. And in the middle of it we'll crawl out, real quiet, and march in among 'em!

Joe.
Huck. } Whoo-pee! If that ain't a great idea!

(They join hands and do a crazy jig)

Joe *(Stopping suddenly)*. Hey! Do you know what?

Tom. What?

Joe. It ain't such a good idea after all.

Tom. Why ain't it?

Joe. After they've finished sobbin' over us, an' kissin' us, and sayin' how glad they are to have us back, they're goin' to start thinkin' of all the trouble they've had draggin' the river an' buyin' funeral clothes an' flowers an' gettin' Reverend Peterson to make up a sermon he ain't able to use. . . . *(He pauses)* They'll skin us alive!

Tom *(Scornfully)*. Don't you think I've thought of that, Joe Harper? Before they kin begin to think o' the trouble we've caused, we'll out with the money an' set their eyes poppin'!

Joe. Then I'm all for it, Tom!

45

Huck. It's a bully idea!

Tom. Then let's divide the booty.

*(***Tom*** puts a couple of bags of coins inside his shirt, and stuffs loose coins in his pockets.* **Joe** *and* **Huck** *do likewise.)*

Joe. Where shall we hide it?

Tom. We'd better stow it in our garbage can 'til we find out whether they're holdin' the service in church or maybe in Judge Thatcher's garden.

Huck. What'd they want to hold it there fer?

Tom. That's where they had it when young Sally Tyson died of the pneumonia. There's three of us, so I reckin they'll have a bigger crowd. *(He puts a few last gold coins in his pocket)* Ready? We want to be in town before sunup.

Joe. I'm ready.

Huck. So am I.

Tom. Then let's go, my hearties! Let's go! *(They file off, whistling)*

Scene 2

(Judge Thatcher's garden the next morning. Near the centre of the stage there is a small table, draped with a black cloth, on which stands a jug of water, a glass, and a bowl of flowers. On either side of the table, at a slight angle to it, there is a row of chairs—about a dozen in all. The fence runs across the back.

As the curtain goes up, **Tom, Joe** *and* **Huck** *creep on stage, and tiptoe over to the table. They look around them. Suddenly,* **Tom** *hears someone coming.)*

Tom. Sssssh!

(They all disappear behind the fence. After a moment the **Minister's Wife** *and* **Widow Douglas** *enter. The* **Widow Douglas** *is carrying a wreath.)*

Minister's Wife. Now, let me see. The Minister asked me to come ahead and see that everything is as he wants it.

Widow Douglas. I suppose he's very much upset by this?

Minister's Wife. Indeed, it's a very sad occurrence.

Widow Douglas. Is there anything I can do to help?

Minister's Wife. I think everything is ready.

Widow Douglas. Will there be enough chairs for the mourners?

Minister's Wife. I doubt it. The others will have to stand. Perhaps we can arrange a few more on the porch. I'll go and see to it.

Widow Douglas. No. Let's sit down just for a moment. There's plenty of time. *(They sit)* Everyone in town will be here, sister. All the schoolchildren. Even the saloons are shut. Even the murder trial is adjourned for the funeral. Poor Mrs Harper. And poor Aunt Polly Sawyer.

Minister's Wife. Indeed, they are to be pitied, Widow Douglas. Yet I feel they are a little to be blamed too.

Widow Douglas. How can you find it in your heart to blame those poor, sorrowing creatures?

Minister's Wife. They should have been more careful of their boys' playfellows. It was that idle, lawless Huckleberry Finn who led those dear, innocent boys astray . . . .

*(*Tom, **Huck** *and* Joe *are listening to all this from behind the fence)*

Widow Douglas. The boy is dead.

Minister's Wife. I am sure it was he who got them to slip out of their beds and go swimming after dark.

Widow Douglas. You have no right to talk that way about the poor, hungry, neglected waif!

Minister's Wife. He was vulgar and bad, and he never went to church.

Widow Douglas. Good, bad or indifferent, Mrs Peterson, he was the Lord's.

Minister's Wife. He didn't even go to school. He smoked. He swore.

Widow Douglas. Yes, and he slept on doorsteps in fine weather and in empty barrels in wet, more shame to us all!

Minister's Wife. I still say they should have forbidden their boys to play with him.

Widow Douglas. So they did. Most mothers in this hard-hearted town did. If the Lord would only give me another chance I'd give that poor, motherless boy a home again under my own roof. I'd put decent clothes on his back and shoes on his feet, and have him educated. . . . (*She wipes away a tear*) As it is I can only give him this wreath.

(**Widow Douglas** *places the wreath in front of the table*)

Minister's Wife. You're a kind-hearted woman, Mrs Douglas.

Widow Douglas. If I'd been a little more kind-hearted when he was alive perhaps this would never have happened. . . .

Minister's Wife (*Comforting her*). There, you mustn't take it so to heart!

(**Mrs Thatcher** *arrives with* **Becky**)

Minister's Wife. Good morning, Mrs Thatcher.

Widow Douglas. Good morning, sister. Good morning, Becky, dear.

Becky (*In tears*). G . . . good morning!

Mrs Thatcher. Sssssh, Becky.

Becky. I can't help it, Ma!

Mrs Thatcher. Control yourself, child.

Widow Douglas. Let the child have her way, Mrs Thatcher. She'll be the better for it. Here, Becky, come and sit with me, and cry your heart out if you feel like it.

(**Becky** *runs over and sits by her*)

Widow Douglas. There, there. . . .

Becky. Oh, Mrs Douglas . . . if I only had . . . had that doorknob again. But I haven't got any . . . anything now to remember Tom by.

Widow Douglas. A doorknob, child?

Becky. It was right out there. But he's gone now. I'll never, never see him any more!

Widow Douglas. I reckon Tom knows you're sorry, Becky.

Becky. I'll never know if he does. He'll never come and ask me to make up again—never, never! I . . . I'm not going to have my party now. I don't want to. Not without Tom.

48

(Mr and Mrs Harper come in)

Minister's Wife *(Going to them).* I thought you and Mr Harper would like to sit right there, Mrs Harper.

Mrs Harper. Thank you.

(They sit to the right of the table)

Minister's Wife. We're waiting for Aunt Polly Sawyer. She's up in Tom's room, poor woman.

Mrs Harper. I know how she feels. You feel nearer to them sitting by their beds.

(Aunt Polly comes in followed by Sid. The Minister's Wife goes forward to comfort her, and leads them to seats on the right of the table.)

Minister's Wife. Everything seems to be ready now. Flowers, water . . . but Judge Thatcher isn't here yet.

Mr Harper. He's down at the courthouse. He'll be here in a while.

Minister's Wife. *(Looking off-stage).* I do believe I can see him coming now. And here's Mr Snodgrass with the poor, dear boys' little playfellows.

(The Schoolmaster arrives ushering in eight or nine boys and girls in their Sunday best)

Minister's Wife. Good morning, Mr Snodgrass.

Schoolmaster *(Raising his hat).* Good morning, ma'am. I trust we're not too late?

Minister's Wife. We're just waiting for Judge Thatcher and then we can begin the service.

Schoolmaster. Ah, this is a terrible thing, ma'am, a terrible thing! That two boys of such promise, such gay high spirits, should be taken away from us. . . . I loved them, ma'am. I loved them as if they were my own. . . .

(One of the Girls gives a little squeal, as the Boy behind her pulls her pigtail)

See me afterwards, Jimmy Slater. 'Vengeance is mine, saith the Lord.' Lead along, children. Boys on the left, girls on the right.

49

(The **Children** *file slowly behind the chairs.* **Judge Thatcher** *comes in.)*

Minister's Wife. You're here, Judge. I'll call my husband and then we can begin.

Judge Thatcher. Just a moment, ma'am. I have a request to make of Miss Sawyer and Mr and Mrs Harper.

Mr Harper. A request, Judge?

Judge Thatcher. Yes. When Muff Potter learned that the court had been adjourned for the funeral of these dear boys, he begged to be allowed to hear the funeral sermon.

Minister's Wife. Muff Potter? The hardened sinner!

Aunt Polly. Let him come if he wants.

Minister's Wife. To profane this sacred service!

Aunt Polly. If that poor, lost creature wants to hear my Tom's funeral service, bring him and let him have his wish. I can't find it in my heart to bear anyone any ill-will today.

Mrs Harper. And neither can I.

Minister's Wife. The Sheriff would have to fetch him, Miss Sawyer. Chains would look mighty queer in this gathering.

Aunt Polly. Let the Sheriff bring him! He loved our boys.

Mrs Harper. Send someone for him, Judge. He's as much right to be present at this service as anyone in town.

Judge Thatcher. Bless you, ma'am! Bless you both! I felt sure you wouldn't refuse so I took the liberty of bringing him with me. *(He calls off-stage)* Bring him in, Sheriff!

(The **Sheriff** *leads in* **Muff Potter,** *in handcuffs)*

Minister's Wife. Well!

Aunt Polly. Come and sit over here by me, Mr Potter.

*(***Muff** *shuffles over and sits by her)*

Well, we're ready to begin.

(The **Minister** *enters. He glances curiously at* **Muff** *and then takes his place by the table.)*

Minister. We will begin this solemn service, dedicated to the memory of our dear departed friends, with a moment's silence . . . .

(The **Grown-ups** *are much affected, and* **Aunt Polly** *wipes away a tear.* **Tom, Joe** *and* **Huck** *watch with real interest. After a minute or so, the* **Minister** *resumes.)*

. . . My friends, we are met here today for a sad purpose. There is not one amongst us who cannot but feel a deep sense of loss. Never were lads of such rare promise cut down in the bloom of their youth. There is not one of us who will not miss their bright faces, there is not man, woman or child who is not the better for having known them. Now, in memory, we see our dear, lost lads as they were. Yes, in our streets their happy laughter and glad voices are still! In the little schoolroom—the little schoolroom they loved so well—there are empty desks. In their homes—alas, their sorrowful homes—there are vacant chairs at table. *(The congregation shows suitable signs of grief)* But in our hearts they are living still. They live in the innumerable good deeds and little acts of kindness and the beautiful and noble incidents of their lives! But look behind you . . . *(No one does)* That plain, board fence, resplendent in its coat of whitewash, that fence, my friends, is a witness to the industry and devotion to duty of brave little Tom Sawyer!

(The **Minister** *pauses for another sip of water.* **Tom** *looks proud, but* **Joe** *and* **Huck** *look at each other in bewilderment.)*

It was less than a week ago, on a Saturday afternoon, that his aunt asked him to perform this task. Did he grumble, did he—as other boys might have done—complain that it was a holiday? No, my friends, he did not!

Aunt Polly *(Weeping).* Oh, I wished I'd have known! I wished I'd known! I'd never have asked him to do it!

Minister. He had planned a jaunt—a harmless little jaunt with his companions, but without grumbling he set to and worked with such a will that, within the afternoon—nay, within the *hour*—he completed it. And there it stands in all its splendour. He needs no monument, my friends, no marble sepulchre! His monument stands here for all to see who pass through our fair town. Let us pray.

(The **Minister** *bows his head in prayer. Everyone else does the same. During the previous speech* **Joe** *and* **Huck,** *who realise now*

51

how **Tom** *has tricked them, have been darting murderous glances
at him. Before they can take any action, however,* **Tom** *signals
them to follow him, and they tiptoe round the fence. They creep
up to the still-praying congregation, and* **Tom** *stands by* **Aunt Polly**
and **Joe** *by* **Mrs Harper.** *At a signal from* **Tom,** *they touch them on
the shoulder.* **Aunt Polly** *and* **Mrs Harper** *look up, cry out, clasp
them to their breast and smother them with kisses. The rest of the
congregation exclaim in amazement. The* **Minister** *stands in
bewilderment for a moment.)*

Minister. 'They that were lost are found'! Praise the Lord! Sing all of
you. Sing a joyful tune!

(The **Minister's Wife** *goes to the house and plays* Praise God from
Whom All Blessings Flow. *Everyone sings.)*

Aunt Polly. Oh Tom, Tom! You're safe, you're safe!

Mrs Harper. My boy, my boy!

Becky *(Flinging her arms round* **Tom's** *neck).* Oh, Tom, it is you.
You're not drowned. You're alive! You're alive!

Tom *(Freeing himself).* Careful, Becky! You're goin' to choke me!

Mrs Harper. We thought you were drowned!

Widow Douglas. And, instead, here they are—safe and sound! Our
prayers have been answered after all. Praise be to God!

Aunt Polly. Amen!

Mrs Harper. But where have you been all this time? The whole village
has been out lookin' for you. . . .

Joe. I know, Ma. You see . . . well, we've been pirates!

Mrs Harper.⎫
Aunt Polly.⎭ Pirates?

Mr Harper. You mean this has all been a . . . a prank, Joe Harper?

Schoolmaster. I thought as much. Truancy!

Aunt Polly. Oh, Tom, how could you? You went near to breakin' my
poor old heart.

Tom. It . . . it wasn't like that, Aunt Polly! Really it wasn't. Joe an'
Huck and me . . . well, we went off to look fer buried treasure on
Jackson's Island. . . . Ain't that right Joe? Huck?

Joe. Sure, we didn't mean no harm, Ma! Huck here found a raft . . . .

Minister's Wife *(Who has just returned from the house).* I knew it! Didn't I say so, Mrs Douglas? Didn't I say that this imp of Satan had led them into mischief?

Widow Douglas. Shame on you, ma'am! I won't hear this poor, innocent creature reviled. . . .

Mr Harper. Innocent! He led our boys into this . . . this disgraceful escapade, didn't he?

Joe. No, pa, he didn't. You won't listen to us. It wasn't Huck's fault. None of it wasn't. It was our fault—Tom's and mine. Ain't that right, Tom?

Tom. That's right, Joe. I was feelin' miserable 'cause Aunt Polly whacked me fer eatin' doughnuts that Sid hooked. . . .

Joe. An' I was feelin' low on account of Ma beatin' me fer stealin' a jug o' cream I never laid eyes on. . . .

Tom. So we decided to hide out on Jackson's Island for a few days an' be pirates an' look for buried treasure. It wasn't Huck's idea. He just decided to come along.

Mrs Harper *(To her husband).* Oh, Henry, we've been too hard on the boy. That cream's been on my conscience ever since I remembered I threw it out 'cause it was sour!

Mr Harper. Well, I don't know. . . .

Widow Douglas. Well, I *do,* Henry Harper! There are some folks as are too ready to blame other folks before they know the facts!

Mr Harper. I reckon you're right, Mrs Douglas. We were a bit too hasty. . . .

Widow Douglas. I should think so!

Mr Harper. What's that you said about treasure, Tom?

Tom. Should I tell them, Joe?

Joe. Now's the time, eh, Huck?

Huck. I guess so.

Tom *(Putting his hand in his pocket and pulling out a handful of coins).* Look at that!

(Everyone crowds round)

Judge Thatcher. Why . . . it's GOLD!

Aunt Polly. Gold? Oh, Tom, what have you been and done?

Tom. Nothin', Aunt—we found it.

Judge Thatcher. Found it?

Tom. Yes, it's buried treasure . . . .

(There are murmurs of 'treasure' *from the astonished onlookers)*

Joe. There's a whole chestful plumb full o' coins like that. Shall I bring it out, Tom?

Tom. Right, Joe!

Judge Thatcher. But I don't understand . . . .

Tom. Just you wait here, Judge Thatcher. All of you wait and we'll bring it out. . . .

(At this precise moment **Injun Joe** *appears. Behind him are four or five other men, with a few women. They are in an angry mood.* **Tom** *stops in his tracks, his face white.)*

Tom. Injun Joe!

Judge Thatcher. Injun Joe! What do you want here?

Minister. If you've come for the funeral service you're too late, my friends.

Injun Joe. We want him.

*(*Injun Joe *points to* Muff Potter*)*

First Man. What's that murderer doin' out of jail?

Second Man. He should be in the courthouse.

Aunt Polly. I said he could come to the service. He's a great friend of the boys and he wanted to pay his last respects. Now, praise God, there's no need.

Third Man. Who let him out?

Judge Thatcher. I did.

Second Man. So the Judge is bein' easy with him, is he?

Injun Joe. That's not my idea of the way to treat a prisoner.

Sheriff. He's safe enough! Look at his chains.

Second Man. Maybe, but we don't like it. . . . He's a murderer. . . .

Judge Thatcher. He's not been tried, Jeff Dolan. That's for the jury to decide.

Third Man. The jury's all here. And we know whether he's guilty or not!

Sheriff. We'd better get him back to the courthouse, Judge.

Judge Thatcher. Yes, I suppose we'd better. Come along, Potter.

First Man. We'll take him along to the courthouse for you, Judge. Just to make sure he doesn't give you the slip on the way.

(There is a burst of laughter from the crowd. The **men** *grab* **Muff***, who is trembling, and push him towards the gate. Suddenly,* **Tom** *calls out.)*

Tom. Stop! Wait! Judge Thatcher, tell them to wait!

Judge Thatcher. What's the matter, boy?

Tom. I . . . I've got somethin' to tell.

Judge Thatcher. Well, what is it?

Tom *(Looking at* **Injun Joe***).* I . . . they . . . .

First Man. Aw, let's get him out of here!

(The **First Man** *pushes* **Muff***)*

Tom. No, you can't! You mustn't!

Judge Thatcher. Speak out. Don't be afraid.

Tom. They mustn't hang Muff, they mustn't!

Judge Thatcher. He hasn't been tried yet.

Tom. You don't understand. He . . . he never killed Dr Robinson. It wasn't Muff. I was there—Huck was there. We both saw it!

Huck *(Shivering with fright).* Oh, you've done it now, Tom! You've gone and broke the oath. We're both done for!

Judge Thatcher. Done for? Oath? I don't understand. . . .

Injun Joe. Are we goin' to waste time listenin' to him?

Second Man. No! Let's get to the courthouse. . . .

Judge Thatcher. Wait a minute. Carry on, Tom.

Tom. We were there. I can prove it. There's a dead cat—an' an oath we wrote not to tell. You can dig it up! I reckon we'll drop dead fer tellin' it, but . . . but it wasn't Muff who did it! It wasn't Muff!

Judge Thatcher. Then who was it?

Tom. I can't tell you. No, sir, neither of us ain't goin' to tell you! Ain't that right, Huck?

*(**Huck** nods dumbly)*

Judge Thatcher. But you must tell me, Tom.

Tom. It ain't no use askin' me, sir. I'm not goin' to tell on anybody. I'm not goin' to tell anythin' except Muff Potter didn't do it! I hope I may never stir if I do!

Judge Thatcher. Tom, the case against Muff is very strong. Nearly everyone believes he killed Dr Robinson. It's no use to keep on saying he didn't do it unless you can prove someone else did it.

Tom. But someone else did! Muff didn't do it!

Judge Thatcher. You were there? Near the grave?

Tom. Yes, sir.

Judge Thatcher. How near?

Tom. About . . . about twelve feet, I guess.

Judge Thatcher. Where were you hiding?

Tom. Behind . . . behind a bush.

Judge Thatcher. You and Huck?

Tom. Yes, the two of us. *(To **Huck**)* I'm sorry, Huck, but I've got to tell. I've got to.

Judge Thatcher. Go on.

Tom. Well, after they'd . . . they'd finished what they were doin' Injun Joe asked Dr Robinson for some more money. I think he said he wanted five dollars. He wouldn't give it him and there was an argument. I couldn't rightly see what happened next, but Dr Robinson hit Injun Joe an' Muff, he said . . . 'Here, don't you hit

56

my pard', and went for the Doc. Then . . . then. . . .

Judge Thatcher. Yes, go on!

Tom. Then . . . Injun Joe picks up Muff's knife from the ground and jammed it into the Doc, and . . .

(**Injun Joe** *suddenly dashes towards* **Tom,** *but is stopped by the* **Sheriff.** *He wriggles free and, pushing his way through the crowd, disappears. There are shouts of* 'Stop him' *and the men, followed by the* **Sheriff,** *dash off after him.*)

Judge Thatcher. Don't panic, folks! They'll get him! *(To* **Muff Potter***)* I reckon I can take these things off now, Muff. *(He unlocks the handcuffs)* You're a free man—thanks to Tom Sawyer.

Muff. I . . . I can't say how grateful I am, Tom. You too, Huck.

Aunt Polly. Oh, I'm so proud of you, Tom!

Tom. It ain't fair! Someone ought to be proud of Huck, too!

Widow Douglas. And so I am! I'm going to take him home with me and see that he never wants for anything! A good home, three meals a day and an education.

Joe *(Pushing his way forward with the box).* Huck don't need any help, ma'am. He's rich!

Widow Douglas. Rich! Well, I never!

Tom. We're all rich! Open the lid an' show 'em Joe!

(**Joe** *flings open the lid. Everyone cranes their necks to see. There are loud* 'oohs!' *and* 'ahhs!'*)*

Aunt Polly. I never did see so much money in all my born days! It's a miracle!

Tom. Now I can buy you that new rockin' chair you've always wanted, Aunt Polly—an' that real crystal vase for the front parlour!

Aunt Polly. Bless you, Tom, bless you!

Judge Thatcher. I guess this calls for a celebration!

Mr Harper. I'm with you there, Judge!

Judge Thatcher. Let's get these chairs cleared. Lend a hand there you children! *(Everyone bustles about clearing the stage, then, to the* **Minister's Wife***)* What about giving us a gay tune on that old piano of yours, ma'am? Something these young people can kick their heels over.

Minister's Wife. I can play *The Dashin' White Sergeant.* [*Or some other appropriate tune*]

Judge Thatcher. Fine! Then *The Dashing White Sergeant* it shall be!

(The **Minister's Wife** *runs off)*

Right! Let's form fours!

(The children form up for the dance)

Huck. Gee, I can't *dance!*

Amy. Course you can! There's nothin' to it. I'll show you.

(**Amy** *pushes him into line)*

Huck. Oh, well . . . !

Judge Thatcher. All ready? Good! Then off we go!

(The children start to dance in time to the piano from off-stage. The **Schoolmaster** *takes a mouth organ from his pocket and accompanies the dancers. The others clap their hands in time to the music. In the middle of the dance the* **Sheriff** *appears pushing in front of him* **Injun Joe,** *his hands tied behind his back. As* **Becky** *and* **Tom** *dance to the front of the stage she speaks to Tom.)*

Becky. You are clever, Tom, finding all that gold!

Tom. Oh, I don't know, Becky, I reckon there's always treasure around if you know where to look for it.